Journey to Easter

Written by Carolyn Bergt

✝

Illustrated by Anton Petrov

CONCORDIA PUBLISHING HOUSE · SAINT LOUIS

Holy Week

PALM SUNDAY

MONDAY

GOOD FRIDAY

Let's take a look at Holy Week,
But in a different way.
Don't stop with sad day number seven.
Let's add one—Easter Day!

We need the start of that next week
To tell all of the story
Of how our Savior died for us
And rose in all His glory.

We can't end with the cross or grave,
So if you calculate
That Christ arose Sunday at dawn,
We really need Day Eight.

Let's have the counting now begin.
Each number tells the news
Of what our Savior did that week
So sin, death, Satan lose.

One Savior, Jesus, True God, Almighty One.

The large crowd that had come to the feast heard that Jesus was coming to Jerusalem. So they took branches of palm trees and went out to meet Him, crying out, "Hosanna! Blessed is He who comes in the name of the Lord, even the King of Israel!"

John 12:12–13

Two elements in the Lord's Supper.

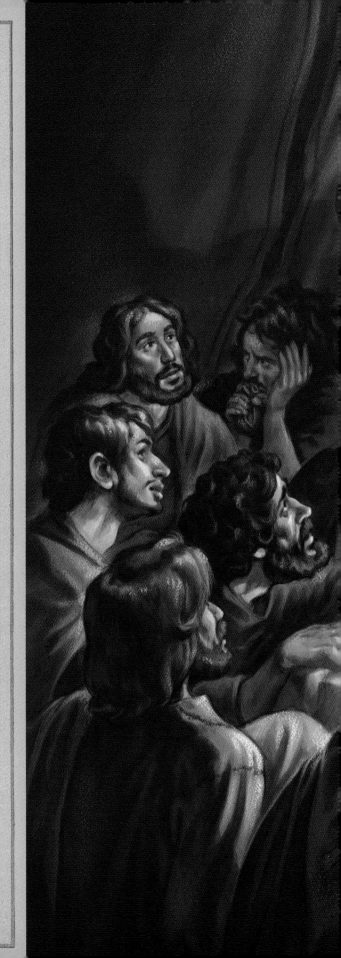

Now as they were eating, Jesus took bread, and after blessing it broke it and gave it to the disciples, and said, "Take, eat; this is My body." And He took a cup, and when He had given thanks He gave it to them, saying, "Drink of it, all of you, for this is My blood of the covenant, which is poured out for many for the forgiveness of sins."
Matthew 26:26–28

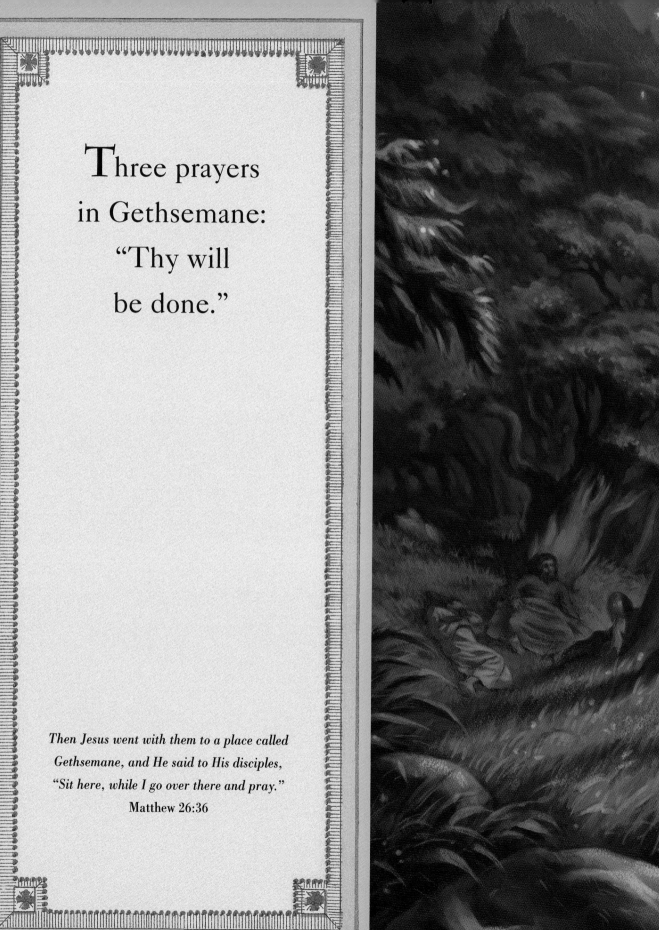

Three prayers in Gethsemane: "Thy will be done."

Then Jesus went with them to a place called Gethsemane, and He said to His disciples, "Sit here, while I go over there and pray."
Matthew 26:36

Four judges
at His trials:
Annas, Caiaphas,
Herod, Pilate.

Pilate said to Him, "So You are a king?"
Jesus answered, "You say that I am a king.
For this purpose I was born and for this purpose
I have come into the world—to bear witness to
the truth. Everyone who is of the truth listens to
My voice." Pilate said to Him, "What is truth?"
John 18:37–38

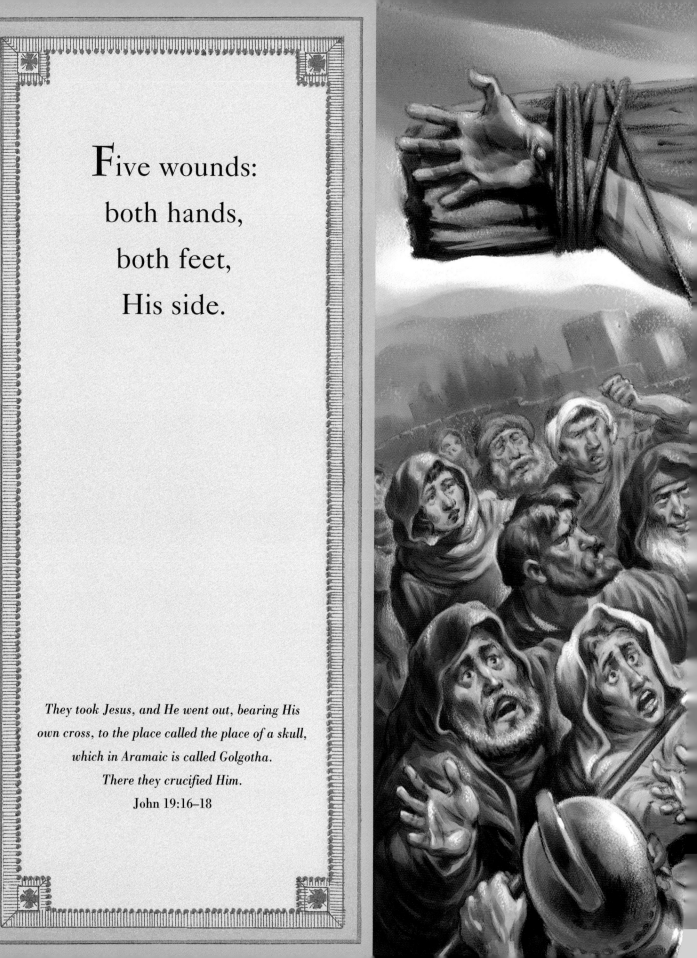

Five wounds:
both hands,
both feet,
His side.

They took Jesus, and He went out, bearing His
own cross, to the place called the place of a skull,
which in Aramaic is called Golgotha.
There they crucified Him.
John 19:16–18

Six hours
on the cross,
suffering,
death.

It was now about the sixth hour,
and there was darkness over the whole land
until the ninth hour, while the sun's light failed.
Luke 23:44–45

Seven times Jesus spoke: He forgave, He finished.

Jesus, calling out with a loud voice, said,
"Father, into Your hands I commit My spirit!"
And having said this He breathed His last.
Now when the centurion saw what
had taken place, he praised God, saying,
"Certainly this man was innocent!"
Luke 23:46–47

We've traveled now through Holy Week.
Each number gave a clue
About how Jesus paid the debt
That for our sin was due.

This task was His, and His alone,
Of this we can be sure,
For only Christ, who is true God,
Can give the sin-sick cure.

Christ Jesus is our substitute.
     He suffered in our place,
And gives His righteousness to us
     With unconditional grace.

The cross is not the story's end.
     Death cannot celebrate.
Let's look ahead to victory
     And that great day—Day Eight.

Eight days—
It's Easter!
His victory
is ours!

Jesus said to her, "Woman, why are you weeping? Whom are you seeking?" Supposing Him to be the gardener, she said to Him, "Sir, if You have carried Him away, tell me where You have laid Him, and I will take Him away." Jesus said to her, "Mary." She turned and said to Him in Aramaic, "Rabboni!" (which means Teacher).
John 20:15–16

Nine kilometers to Emmaus—about the distance Jesus walked and talked with friends that same day.

Beginning with Moses and all the Prophets,
He interpreted to them in all the Scriptures
the things concerning Himself.
Luke 24:27

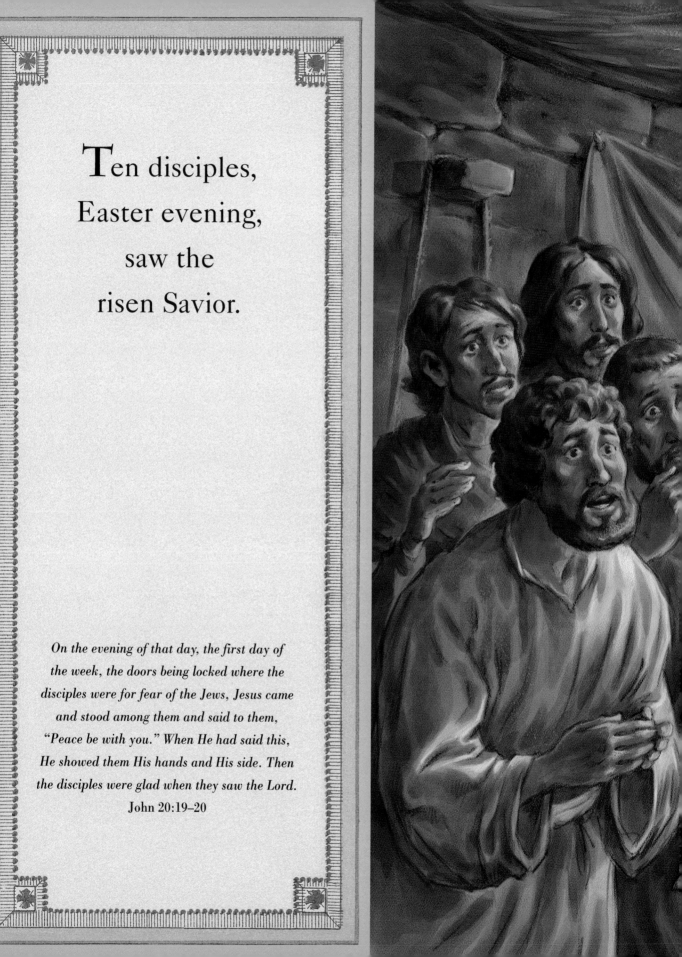

Ten disciples, Easter evening, saw the risen Savior.

On the evening of that day, the first day of the week, the doors being locked where the disciples were for fear of the Jews, Jesus came and stood among them and said to them, "Peace be with you." When He had said this, He showed them His hands and His side. Then the disciples were glad when they saw the Lord.
John 20:19–20

When Christ the Lord died on the cross,
The day was filled with gloom.
They buried Him, but death could not
Hold God inside that tomb.

The promise Jesus often made
Came true, for He arose!
He lives again! He's conquered sin
And all our greatest foes!

Christ Jesus lives, we know it's so,
  The Bible says it's true.
He's present in His Holy Meal
  And Holy Baptism too.

He lives for us—we live for Him.
  He gives to us—we praise.
On Easter and each Sunday too
  Our alleluias raise.

Christ is risen!
He is risen indeed!
Alleluia!

*They devoted themselves to the apostles'
teaching and fellowship, to the breaking
of bread and the prayers.*
Acts 2:42

Published by Concordia Publishing House
3558 S. Jefferson Avenue, St. Louis, MO 63118-3968

Text copyright © 2004 Concordia Publishing House

Illustrations copyright © 2004 Anton Petrov

Manufactured in the United States of America

1 2 3 4 5 6 7 8 9 10   13 12 11 10 09 08 07 06 05 04